The Millie Ola Children's Book Series

A, B, C...

Says OlaRose

By
Olachi Mezu-Ndubuisi

BLACK ACADEMY PRESS, INC.

Millie Ola Children's Book Series

By Olachi Mezu-Ndubuisi
BLACK ACADEMY PRESS, INC.
4015 Old Court Road,
Pikesville, Maryland 21208

Copyright ©2016 Black Academy Press Inc.
Written and created by Olachi Mezu Ndubuisi
Illustrated by Cam

First Published in USA in 2009
By Black Academy Press, Inc.
www.blackacademypress.com
2nd edition printed in 2016

Printed in the U.S.A
ISBN: 0-87831-139-4   978-0-87831-139-2

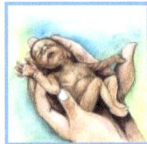

Book sales will go to the ObiOlaRose Twin Angels Foundation to help support parents of premature and sick infants and neonatal services in underserved areas.
www.obiolarosefoundation.org

Dedication

To my miracle baby, OlaRose, who was born early. You are my inspiration, source of strength, and God's most precious gift to me.

This book belongs to

_____

Please read it to me.

A is for Ape,

it lives in the trees.

It will jump and gape
if you talk and stare.

B is for bat,
it flies in the dark.
It is blind, you know that
and will miss the mark.

C is for camel,
it has a hump.
It is one mammal
whose back has a bump.

D is for donkey,

it has long ears.

It brays with a low key,

and has no cares

E is for elephant,

it has tusks near his nose.

It makes a noise when you rant

and has such huge toes.

F is for frog,

it lives in a pond.

It can eat a bug

with its sticky tongue.

G is for giraffe,

it has a neck so long.

It never has enough

to chew all day long.

H is for hen,

it loves to lay eggs.

Sometimes ten or more

hatch into chicks with legs.

I is for iguana,

it is a reptile.

It's not much of a runner

with four legs and a tail.

J is for Jaguar,

the big cat of the pack.

Known for its fierce manner,

it can jump to attack.

K is for kangaroo,

it has a pouch so deep

it's warm and not too cool

for its baby to sleep.

L is for lion,
it roars out loud.
As strong as iron,
it is fierce and proud.

M is for monkey,
it is cute and hairy,
It's so fun to see
'cos it's so merry

N is for newt,

it has four legs.

For sure it's so cute

as it runs and lays eggs.

O is for owl,

it keeps awake at night,

to hoot aloud and howl

till it's dawn and light.

P is for parrot.

it talks a lot and causes a riot

when it says

what you'd rather not.

Q is for quail,

that's a bird with wings.

It will never fail

to flap in the winds.

R is for rat,

it likes to eat cheese.

That makes it fat,

but it still runs with ease.

S is for swan,

it is full of elegance.

It cares not if you're a fan

of its graceful neck and stance.

T is for tortoise,

it has a hard shell.

It walks so slowly with poise

so its plan, none can tell.

U is for unicorn,
a mythical horse it is.
It indeed has one horn
a true beauty for one to see.

V is for Vulture,

who eats between its meals.

With a bald head for sure

I wonder how it feels.

W is for Whale,

it lives in the ocean.

It will never ever fail

to flap its tail in motion.

X is for Xiphias,
it is a swordfish.
Its jaw no-one dares
to touch in its niche.

Y is for Yak,

it loves to eat grass.

It sure makes its mark,

when it chews as you pass.

Z is for Zebra,

it has white and black colors.

It's as graceful as an opera

that sings in colors.

I know my ABC

I know my animals

I know my animals in ABC,

says OlaRose.

A B C D E
F G H I J
K L M N O
P Q R S T
U V W X Y
Z 1 2 3 4

Yes I know my ABC
I know my animals in
ABC, says OlaRose.
But do you know your
1,2,3 Says OlaRose

Millie Ola Children's Book Series

About the Book

A,B,C , Says OlaRose is one of the books in the Says OlaRose Collection of the Millie Ola Children's Book Series. Other titles in the series are : 1,2,3.. says OlaRose and Born Early, Says OlaRose: The story of OlaRose & Obiola.

About The Author

Olachi Mezu-Ndubuisi *aka* Millie Ola is an optometrist, neonatologist, research scientist and mother of premature one pound daughter, OlaRose, who uses her love for writing to follow, nurture and cherish her daughter's development.

Book sales will go to the ObiOlaRose Twin Angels Foundation to help support parents of premature and sick infants and neonatal services in underserved areas.

www.obiolarosefoundation.org

9 780878 311392

www.ingramcontent.com/pod-product-compliance
Lightning Source LLC
Chambersburg PA
CBHW041818040426
42452CB00001B/11